every teen girl's little pink book on gab

by Cathy Bartel

Harrison House
Tulsa, Oklahoma

10 09 08 07 06   10 9 8 7 6 5 4 3 2 1

every teen girl's little pink book on gab
ISBN 13: 978-1-57794-793-6
ISBN 10: 1-57794-793-2
Copyright © 2006 by Cathy Bartel
P.O. Box 691923
Tulsa, Oklahoma 74179

Published by Harrison House, Inc.
P.O. Box 35035
Tulsa, Oklahoma 74153

contents

girls
about to
become

Girls like to gab, and gab is great because all that talking is what makes you who you are! If what you think about, you talk about and bring about, then what you say is very important. You can make the most of your words in every situation. Talking and sharing with your friends and family is fun. Discover how to be heard, enjoyed, and respected for what you say and who you are!

the gift
of gab

Have you ever heard the term "the gift of gab"? Gab isn't always a gift! But it can be when we use our mouths to bless. The Bible says that when we speak, we either speak life or death. Our words are containers of power for good or for evil! I want to use my mouth for good, and I know you do too.

Life and death are in the power of the tongue. I have to say, that is one powerful little muscle in our mouth, and we absolutely need to exercise control over it! Now, how do we do that?

Well, we need to ask the Lord to help us. For example, you can say, "Lord, help me to say good and kind words to everyone in my life."

Guess what? Included in that *everyone* is you! You have got to talk about yourself and to yourself in a good and kind way! You need to encourage your friends, your family, *and* yourself with God's Word.

A bit in the mouth of a horse controls the whole horse. A small rudder on a huge ship in the hands of a skilled captain sets a course in the face of the strongest winds. A word out of your mouth may seem of no account, but it can accomplish nearly anything—or destroy it! It only takes a spark, remember, to set off a forest fire.

James 3:3-5 MSG

Take charge! Think before you speak!

Now, let me be the first to tell you right here and now that I am so thankful to God for forgiveness. In the past, my gab has not always been good gab. We all have areas in our lives where we are growing and changing. When we confess our sin, our heavenly Father is so faithful to forgive us and give us a new beginning. He makes our sin-stained hearts as white as snow!

Our speech is something we will have to work on for the rest of our lives. We can't let our guard down. We've got to stay on our toes. We just need to daily ask the Lord for help to use our words wisely.

When I was about 11, 12, and 13 years old, I was a "cusser." I'm not proud to tell you that, but I share it with you for a reason. When I asked Jesus to come into my heart, it was like He took a bar of soap and washed my mouth out! One day I had some really bad gab coming out of my mouth; the next day it was gone! That made me so happy, and it was a very obvious change to my friends. I have never had a desire to cuss since.

I am so thankful I don't say those words anymore. That wouldn't be appropriate for a pastor's wife! Really, it's not attractive for any young woman to speak like that.

> Watch the way you talk. Let nothing foul or dirty come out of your mouth. Say only what helps, each word a gift. Don't grieve God. Don't break his heart. His Holy Spirit, moving and breathing in you, is the most intimate part of your life, making you fit for himself. Don't take such a gift for granted.

> *Ephesians 4:29,30 MSG*

This Scripture isn't just talking about cussing. I believe it's talking about gossiping, backbiting, telling dirty jokes, and even complaining.

Proverbs 16:28 says that gossip separates the best of friends. Don't you know that if you have a friend that is always gossiping about other people, there's a big chance she's talking about you when you're not around?

We all need to check up on ourselves and have a little mouth-washing ceremony once in a while. Just as we can whiten our teeth, we can whiten what comes out of our mouths!

If you are having trouble with your mouth, you can do these things to get it clean again.

Pray. The Lord will help you if you ask Him to.

Ask a friend to help you. Make yourself account-able to a friend. Tell your sins to each other, and pray for each other so you may be healed. "The prayer of a person living right with God is something powerful and to be reckoned with" (James 5:16 MSG).

Always trust the Lord to help you conquer bad habits and develop new habits in every area of your life. Say this: "I can do all things through Christ who strengthens me" (Phil. 4:13 NKJV).

think pink

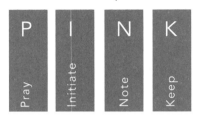

PROVERBS
15:1 NKJV

A soft answer turns away
wrath, but a harsh word
stirs up anger.

Conversation is an
exercise of the mind;
gossip is merely an
exercise of the tongue.

—Author Unknown[i]

gossip

A false witness will not go unpunished, and he who speaks lies shall perish.

Proverbs 19:9 NKJV

A man gossiped about his friend. Soon his friend confronted him, and the gossiper became very sorrowful for the wrong he had done. He asked for his friend's forgiveness, which he granted, and asked if he could do anything to make things right between them. The friend said, "Take two down pillows and go to the center of town; cut the pillows open and wave them in the air till the feathers are all out. Then come back and see me."

The man did just as he'd been told and came back to his friend. The friend said, "I've forgiven you. But to realize how much harm your gossiping has caused me, go back to the center of town and collect all the feathers." The man regretfully realized it would be impossible to find and collect every feather.

Gossip hurts people, destroys relationships, and harms the gossiper. Gossiping causes people to distrust you. They are thinking in the back of their minds, *If she gossips about this person behind her back, what is she saying about me behind mine?* Respect yourself and others: Don't gossip.

details,
details

Girls are detailed.
We love to know exactly what happened when our best friend got her driver's license or when she had her hair done. And we want to tell every detail when something happens to us.

The benefit of all those thoughts and details is that we consider all the aspects of a problem before we decide on a solution. The negative is that we sometimes have trouble deciding what to do because we are considering so much information. You've probably heard the saying, "It's a girl's prerogative to change her mind," and that's right because we have so many different options!

The challenge is keeping our foot out of our mouth and staying focused. We are so tempted to just blurt out those thoughts before considering what we are going to say.

Proverbs shows us that when we hold our tongue we are wise.

When words are many, sin is not absent,
but he who holds his tongue is wise.

Proverbs 10:19 *NIV*

We can all learn from that one, huh? Think of a time recently when you wish you would have held your tongue. Would you have been seen as wise instead of foolish?

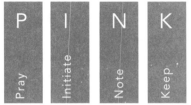

P Pray
I Initiate
N Note
K Keep.

PROVERBS 21:9 AMP

a girl no one wants to marry
(or even date!)

It is better to dwell in a corner of the
housetop [on the flat oriental roof,
exposed to all kinds of weather] than
in a house shared with a nagging,
quarrelsome, and faultfinding woman.

The best way to cheer yourself is to try to cheer someone else up.

—Mark Twain[ii]

6 gabs to avoid

We have all been in relationships in which we thought someone was our true friend and then down the road realized she wasn't. A true friend doesn't just call herself a friend, but backs up her words with action. Check out the gab from these 6 so-called "friends," and learn to avoid them.

1. Backstabber

This is someone who talks one way in front of you, but says something totally different behind your back. A backstabber cannot be trusted by anyone.

2. User

The user is just looking for a temporary friend. This person will sweet-talk you for personal gain and then toss you out like a dirty dishrag.

3. Control freak

"It's my way or the highway," this one will say. The control freak will not compromise. You're only going and doing what this person wants to do. Your opinion doesn't matter.

4. Manipulator

If you don't want to do what the manipulator wants you to do, this person will find a way to convince you to do it her way. The manipulator is sly and will influence you to do things you never thought you would do—all for her own selfish ambitions.

5. Moocher

This person wants you to provide for her every need. "Can I borrow your clothes?" "Can I borrow your car?" "Can I borrow a couple of bucks?" As you give, you'll never receive anything in return.

6. Complainer

You can never please the complainer no matter what you do. If you gave this person a $100 bill, she would complain because it's not two $50 bills. Save yourself, and avoid this one.

gab test

Gab can be a curse or a gift, depending on how we choose to use it. When we say the right thing at the right time, our words can actually soothe people and bring healing. Good and kind words can change someone's life.

Let's take a moment and do a little heart checkup. Be very honest with yourself as you go through these questions.

1. *Am I a **blabber gabber**?*

Definition: One who gossips and spreads rumors, always saying something negative about her family and friends.

Yes   No   Sometimes

2. *Am I a **crabby gabby**?*

Definition: One who is constantly grumbling and complaining about everything. One who is mad at the world, bent out of shape, bitter, and cranky.

Yes   No   Sometimes

 *Am I a **drab gab**?*

Definition: One who is always talking about negative, depressing things. One who sees the glass half-empty and sounds a lot like Eeyore.

Yes   No   Sometimes

 *Am I a **jab gab**?*

Definition: One who continually pokes fun at people. One who feels better about oneself by making fun of people.

Yes   No   Sometimes

 *Am I a **stab gab**? Ouch!*

Definition: One who stabs people in the back with words. Very "mean girls" do this!

It's brutal, dangerous, hurts a lot, and is very deceptive!

Yes   No   Sometimes

Am I a **tabs gab?**

Definition: One who puts her nose in everyone's business. One who feels it is her responsibility to keep tabs on everyone and let everyone else know about it. Also known as a busybody gab.

Yes   No   Sometimes

Am I a **fab gab?**

Definition: One who uses gab to encourage, build up, give life, kindness, and wisdom. This is delightful, beautiful, and extremely pleasing!

Yes   Yes   Yes

think pink

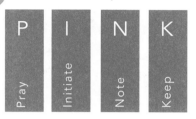

PINK

Pray
Initiate
Note
Keep

1 THESSALONIANS
5 : 14 M S G

*Gently encourage the stragglers,
and reach out for the exhausted,
pulling them to their feet.
Be patient with each person,
attentive to individual needs.*

"Watch your thoughts; they become your words. Watch your words; they become your actions. Watch your actions; they become your habits. Watch your habits; they become your character. Watch your character for it will become your destiny."

—Frank Outlaw[iii]

gabsters

Most girls like to talk a lot, and God made us that way on purpose. We're gabsters! We think with both sides of our brain, so we have lots of thoughts: some creative, some logical, some that make sense, and some that don't! With all those thoughts rolling around in our heads, it's easy to speak out. That can help us or can work against us. Let me share with you some great ways to let those words work for you.

> Death and life are in the power of the tongue, and they who indulge in it shall eat the fruit of it [for death or life].
>
> *Proverbs 18:21 AMP*

We can speak good things out of our mouths and, as a result, enjoy good things in our lives. But if we speak negative things, we can generate negative results in our lives.

Who would think that words could affect your life so much? But it's true. Your words count. Make it a habit to *speak life*. Speak good things. Sometimes that's hard, especially when you are faced with a difficult circumstance. You might want to just complain or cry, but if you can find a positive Scripture to say in that situation instead, you will be on the path to success.

Here's one Scripture to keep in your memory next time you feel overwhelmed.

> You, dear children, are from God and have overcome them, because the one who is in you is greater than the one who is in the world.
>
> 1 John 4:4 NIV

Let God's Word be your motto in tough times, and enjoy the benefits of good words!

think pink

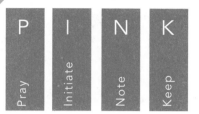

P — Pray
I — Initiate
N — Note
K — Keep

PROVERBS
25:11 AMP

A word fitly spoken and in
due season is like apples of
gold in settings of silver.

The reason a dog has so many friends is that he wags his tail instead of his tongue.

—Author Unknown

lift

Do not be deceived, God is not mocked; for whatever a man sows, that he will also reap.

Galatians 6:7 NKJV

Look at some of these creative cut-downs, and see if you have ever been guilty of using them:

 "You got into the gene pool when the lifeguard wasn't watching."

 "If I gave you a penny for your thoughts, you'd get change."

 "When you open your mouth, it's only to change whatever foot was previously in there."

 Small people cut others down to feel good about themselves. A person with a healthy self-esteem doesn't need to.

 If you want to feel good, help someone else feel good. Reach out. Be a friend. Give a kind word. Be the bigger person: Lift others up to your level rather than cutting them down.

chatty cathy

When I was a little girl, I had a doll named Chatty Cathy. (She's sold in antique stores now. Ouch!) Anyway, I would pull her string and she would "chat": "Hi, I'm Chatty Cathy. How are you today? I love you!" and so on. My mom told me that I went through a couple of those dolls because I would wear them right out.

I guess most of us girls need to get control of *our* string and give *our* voice a rest, so we don't wear ourselves and others out!

When my husband is watching something on TV (usually a football or hockey game) and doesn't want to be disturbed, he's been known to try to mute me with the remote when I try to chat. That's not very nice, is it?

But it really is something to think about. We really can't mute ourselves with an electronic device. Therefore, our only option is self-control, not a remote control!

think pink

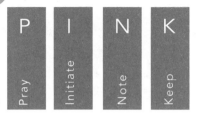

P Pray
I Initiate
N Note
K Keep

PSALM 141:3,4 MSG

Post a guard at my mouth, God, set a watch at the door of my lips. Don't let me so much as dream of evil or thoughtlessly fall into bad company. And these people who only do wrong—don't let them lure me with their sweet talk!

There are people who, instead of listening to what is being said to them, are already listening to what they are going to say themselves.

—Albert Guinon[iv]

Little Pink Book on Gab

control

For in many things we offend all. If any man offend not in word, the same is a perfect man, and able also to bridle the whole body.

James 3:2

This verse says that by controlling the tongue, we are able to control the desires and impulses of the entire body.

We live in a body that has fleshly desires and wants to commit stupid sins. The way we will be able to control these desires is by speaking the right words. If we talk about sex all the time, guess what we're going to do really soon?

Our words will guide and direct our life, so we need to weigh each one carefully and let the Word of God be a regular part of our vocabulary.

2 ears—
1 mouth

Have you ever noticed that when we girls get together, we can talk so fast and furious? We are known for this.

Sometimes when I'm with a group of ladies and we're just visiting, someone may tell a story that triggers a story that I want to tell. I find myself just wanting to get my turn in. I have had to tell myself, "Calm down, Cathy. Don't be rude." I hate when I have interrupted someone out of just plain rudeness.

We all like to get our 2 cents in. It's so much fun to get together with our friends, but we really have to remember to bring our manners with us.

When my boys were little and we were going somewhere, I'd say right before we'd get out of the car, "Did you bring your manners? Okay, let's put them on!"

Have you ever left somewhere and just kicked yourself all the way home because you got carried away in your conversation? I've done that, and I'm very thankful for God's forgiveness. I've learned that I sure save myself a lot of trouble when I think before I speak.

We need to keep this Scripture in our hearts and do it:

> Don't think only about your own affairs, but be interested in others, too, and what they are doing.
>
> *Philippians 2:4 NLT*

Remember: 2 ears, 1 mouth. God gave us 2 ears so we could listen twice as much as we speak. We'll be amazed at how much we can learn if we just make a point to listen once in a while. This takes practice if we're not used to it, but I know we can all learn to be good listeners.

think pink

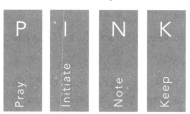

P **I** **N** **K**

Pray — Initiate — Note — Keep

PROVERBS
17 : 28   N K J V

Even a fool is counted wise when he
holds his peace; when he shuts his lips,
he is considered perceptive.

Men are born with two
eyes, but only one tongue,
in order that they should
see twice as much
as they say.

—Charles Caleb Colton[v]

listen up

A great American leadership and management trainer recently said, "In hundreds of interviews with people at all levels, I've made this discovery: The bigger the person, the more apt he is to encourage you to talk; the smaller the person, the more apt he is to preach to you. Big people monopolize the listening; small people monopolize the talking!"

There's a reason God gave us 2 ears and 1 mouth. Good leaders are great listeners, as are good friends. Are you more concerned with hearing or being heard?

gab about everyone!

guys

God put it in you to be attracted to guys. Just don't go overboard in your thoughts and words. Guys aren't everything (even though they may seem to be). The guys you know today might not even cross your mind in 2 or 3 years. Hold out for God's best. Don't commit too much.

After Eve was deceived by Satan in the Garden of Eden, the Lord said to her, "Your desire will be for your husband, and he will rule over you" (Gen. 3:16 NIV). Since that desire is in you, keep tabs on it. You can control your thoughts and emotions and save the best for the man you marry.

friends

Proverbs 18:24 NLT says, "There are 'friends' who destroy each other, but a real friend sticks closer than a brother."

A true friend sticks closer than a brother or sister. That means true friends don't slice and dice each other with their words. Maybe you and your friends tore each other down in fourth grade, but now you're making friends for life. Words can hurt, or words can heal. When you have friends, you stick by each other—especially with your words.

teachers

Seems like you either love them or, uh, are challenged with them. You can find favor with either kind of teacher—even the most difficult one. If you say positive things over your relationships with teachers and keep yourself from talking them down with your friends, you can build favor for yourself. It might be tough to keep it quiet, especially when you'd like to rip those teachers to shreds, but you will win in the long run if you keep the trash talk out of your life.

> Let not mercy and truth forsake you; bind them around your neck, write them on the tablet of your heart, and so find favor and high esteem in the sight of God and man.
>
> Proverbs 3:3,4 NKJV

You can place "teacher" in that verse instead of "man." What teacher can you pray that Scripture over? I do it like this:

Father God, I thank You that I am merciful and truthful and that I have favor in Your sight and with my teachers, in Jesus' name.

parents

The Word of God tells us that we should honor our parents. Of the Ten Commandments, it's the first one with a promise. That promise is a long life!

Children, obey your parents in the Lord, for this is right. "Honor your father and mother," which is the first command-ment with promise: "that it may be well with you and you may live long on the earth."

Ephesians 6:1-3 NKJV

How do you honor your parents? Is it just doing what they say? Actually, that word "honor" in the *Amplified Bible* version is to "esteem and value as precious." That means your attitude matters too. You honor them by keeping a good attitude even when you don't want to. A good attitude includes saying good words about them. You can do it! It's worth a long life, and you'll win big points with your parents and God.

think pink

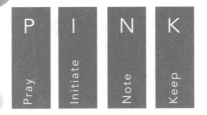

P Pray
I Initiate
N Note
K Keep

COLOSSIANS
14:6 NIV

Let your conversation be always full of grace, seasoned with salt, so that you may know how to answer everyone.

Always attempt to be mannerly and gracious, seeking never to offend in word or deed, always considering the feelings of others.

—Sharon Daugherty[vi]

If you can't say
something nice, don't say
nothing at all!

—Thumper

3 things to gab with your parents

Communication is the key to victory in any kind of relationship. Great companies, great armies, great churches, great sports teams, and great homes all have 1 thing in common: They have learned to communicate effectively with one another. Communication is not just talking. It is listening, observing, studying, and, finally, talking. People who only learn to talk are not communicating; they are spewing. In opening up good communication lines with your parents, there are 3 things you must always tell them.

 1. *Tell them when you need help.*

It may be in school, a relationship, or a job, but if you need help and guidance, let your parents know. That's why God gave them to you: to help you get through tough times.

2. *Tell them when you've made a mistake.*

It might be easier at the time to try to cover it up. However, honesty not only will help you avoid making this same mistake again; it will also earn you big points in the "trust" quest.

3. *Tell them you love and appreciate them.*

Sure, there's no such thing as a perfect parent, but most all have made a very significant investment of time, energy, and money in their children. Regularly let yours know you love them, even if they don't always show the same love in return.

good gab
(the best
gab of all)

There is one type of gab that is in a category of its own. It's the kind of gab that we can only experience with God, and it is the most powerful thing we can do with our mouths. When we talk with God and thank Him, and when we remind Him of His words to us, our mouths are being used to accomplish His will in this world.

As we spend time with Jesus, it will be very evident to others that we've been in His presence by how we speak.

For example:

> When we take time to worship the Lord and thank Him for all He's doing in our lives, our conversations with others begin to show that we have a thankful heart. "I will bless the Lord at all times; His praise will continually come out of my mouth" (Ps. 34:1).

> When we cast our cares on the Lord, as He has asked us to, our words will be full of faith

and confidence rather than dread and worry. Our help comes from the Lord, and when we give our care to Him we are assured that He will take care of us. (Ps. 121:2; 1 Peter 5:7.)

When we ask for forgiveness (a very important part of prayer), we are forgiven! The Bible says that when we confess (with our mouths) our sins, God is faithful and just to forgive us and to cleanse us from all unrighteousness. That means we are in right standing with Him. That sin is washed away. When we receive forgiveness, we are able to hold our heads up and, therefore, able to look into other people's eyes and speak to them of God's love and mercy. Our words will bring joy and peace to people in our lives.

The Lord has called us as His daughters to stand in the gap for others. What a privilege to pray for others to receive salvation! Now, that is the most wonderful way to make ourselves and our mouths available to God.

Prayer heals broken hearts, sets people free from addictions, opens people's eyes to the truth, and makes them whole in their spirit, soul, and body.

I'm so thankful for the people who have prayed for you and me and our loved ones. Let's always be thoughtful and ready to pray for others.

think pink

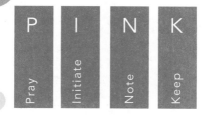

P — Pray
I — Initiate
N — Note
K — Keep

PROVERBS 16:23

*I think before I speak
because the mind of the wise
instructs her mouth.*

A slip of the foot you may soon recover, but a slip of the tongue you may never get over.

—Benjamin Franklin[vii]

meditate

Let the words of my mouth, and the meditation of my heart, be acceptable in thy sight, O Lord, my strength, and my redeemer.

Psalm 19:14

This Scripture ties the words of our mouths to the meditations of our hearts. See, whatever we think about is what we're going to be talking about with our mouths. Of course, there are always a few in every crowd who fail to think at all before they talk, but for the most part our mouths follow our thoughts.

When someone talks about meditation, the image that usually surfaces in our minds is a Chinese-looking guy in a toga, sitting cross-legged, his eyes closed and his fingers in circles, humming in G minor. (At least it does in my imagination.)

However, to His eternal credit, this is not what God has in mind when He tells us to meditate. He's simply asking us to take a few extra moments in our day to really think about and mull over His Word.

When you do, you'll gain new revelation and better understanding about how to make it work in your life.

C'mon—try it.

believe in your gab

Another word to describe a "Christian," or follower of Jesus Christ, is "believer."

We should be called "believers" because we believe that Jesus Christ is the Son of God and have accepted Him as our Lord. Believers believe. It's important that we believe in what we say, just as we believe in Jesus Christ. Jesus tells us this in the book of Mark.

> "For assuredly, I say to you, whoever says to this mountain, 'Be removed and be cast into the sea,' and does not doubt in his heart, but believes that those things he says will be done, he will have whatever he says. Therefore I say to you, whatever things you ask when you pray, believe that you receive them, and you will have them."

Mark 11:23,24 NKJV

When we pray, if we believe that we receive what we ask for, Jesus says we will indeed receive them. But if you say things that are not true most of time, then when it comes time to pray, it's pretty tough to believe that you'll get what you ask for. When your words are messed up, your believer is all messed up! Your spiritual side doesn't know when to believe or when not to believe.

Have you ever known someone who just seemed to lie about everything? You couldn't trust them. It's the same with your spiritual side. If you mix up your words with some truth and some other stuff, you can't trust yourself when you pray. Remember the quote from Shakespeare's play *Hamlet:* "To thine own self be true."

In the book of Hebrews, the writer tells us that the children of Israel did not enter the Promised Land because they had an unbelieving heart. (Heb. 3:7-12.) Don't let an unbelieving heart stop you from receiving God's best. If you ask the Lord to help you, He'll let you know on the inside when you've crossed over the line of unbelief with your words. Then you can correct it right then. That will keep your believer strong!

think pink

P I N K

Pray | Initiate | Note | Keep

HEBREWS 4:14 NKJV

Seeing then that we have a great High Priest who has passed through the heavens, Jesus the Son of God, let us hold fast our confession.

Father God, I am a believer and stand strong in my declaration of faith. You are my very present help in trouble. You guide me and lead me into all truth. You cause my thoughts to become agreeable to Your will, and so my plans are established and succeed, in Jesus' name. Amen.

Wise men speak because they have something to say; Fools because they have to say something.

—Plato[viii]

3 things to erase from your thoughts and gab

The Bible teaches us in 2 Corinthians 10:5 to cast down every high thought that would try to exalt itself against the knowledge of God. The act of casting down must be aggressive, and it must be followed with intentionally thinking what will encourage your walk with Christ. Guard carefully against the following thoughts, because they turn into words.

"No one cares about you."

This thought tempts us towards self-pity, but it is a lie. People do care and, most importantly, God cares! Say out loud, "God cares about me, and people care about me."

"You won't succeed."

You have every reason to be confident of success if you are walking with God. Philippians 4:13 says you can do all things though Christ who strengthens you. Say out loud, "I will succeed in life. Jesus Christ strengthens my spirit, soul, and body."

3. "Just give up."

Jesus didn't quit on you. He doesn't have a quitting spirit, and He didn't put a quitting spirit in you. Persevere and finish the race! Say out loud, "I will not quit. I have a strong spirit. I will find my destiny, and I will finish my course."

get what you gab

The same way you received Jesus as your Lord is the same way you receive all things from God. You say, "Jesus, come into my life. I believe You are the Son of God and that You died for my sins and rose again." You find this in the book of Romans:

> That if you confess with your mouth, "Jesus is Lord," and believe in your heart that God raised him from the dead, you will be saved. For it is with your heart that you believe and are justified, and it is with your mouth that you confess and are saved.

Romans 10:9,10 NIV

This principle of believing with your heart and saying with your mouth is how you receive from God. If you are sick and need to be healed, you can find a Scripture in the Bible that says you are healed. For instance, 1 Peter 2:24 says that by the stripes of Jesus you are healed. You believe that Scripture is true for you, and then you say that Scripture over your life. Words and thoughts are important to God. He made an easy way for you to connect with Him and change the circumstances in your life: talk!

think pink

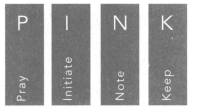

P — Pray
I — Initiate
N — Note
K — Keep

HEBREWS 11:3 NLV

Through faith we understand that the world was made by the Word of God. Things we see were made from what could not be seen.

When God created the world, He used words. When He spoke, things happened. God said, "Let there be light," and light was. God said, "Let the earth bring forth living creatures," and animals appeared. His words caused the science of this world to form.

In the same way, your words can affect your world. Keep your words positive, and speak life!

Just as God created the world with words, you and I can create our world around us by the words of our mouth.

—Kate McVeigh[ix]

7 words to remove from your gab

 "Can't."

You can do all things through Christ who strengthens you. (Phil. 4:13.)

 "Never."

All things are possible to those who believe. (Mark 9:23.)

 "Quit."

"Let us not grow weary while doing good, for in due season we shall reap if we do not lose heart" (Gal. 6:9 NKJV).

 "Depressed."

"Rejoice in the Lord always: and again I say, Rejoice" (Phil. 4:4).

 "Hate."

The Holy Ghost sheds the love of God abroad in our hearts. (Rom. 5:5.)

6. *"Doubt."*

"So then faith comes by hearing, and hearing by the word of God" (Rom. 10:17 NKJV).

 7. *"Broke."*

My God shall supply all of your needs by His riches in glory in Christ Jesus. (Phil. 4:19.)

kind gab

Psalm 45:1 says that our tongue is as the pen of a ready writer. The book of Proverbs says we are to write God's Word on the tablet of our hearts. Let's use our tongues to write God's love on people's hearts.

In Proverbs 31, the Bible tells us about a woman who is very wise. It says that when she speaks, she always has something worthwhile to say and she always says it kindly. When she opens her mouth she shares wisdom, and the law of kindness is on her tongue. I just want to encourage you that you are very capable of being that young Proverbs 31 woman.

If you haven't taken charge of your tongue, begin right now. There is no telling how many lives you can help and bless by speaking life-giving words. The bottom line is that our words help bring people closer to the Lord.

We have good news to share with people. We can't leave it all up to the preachers. There are people who won't give any preacher the time of day, but will listen to your testimony. There are people who won't otherwise step foot in a church, but will one day to hear your pastor or youth pastor because you opened your mouth and lovingly invited them to come with you. The next thing you know, they will have received Jesus into their hearts because you reached out with a wise and kind word. I'd say that's using your gab as a gift! The best gift of all—salvation!

Proverbs 11:30 says the fruit of those who are right with God is a tree of life, and he who wins souls is wise!

think pink

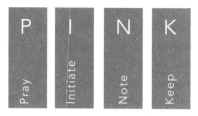

P I N K

Pray Initiate Note Keep

Make an effort today to minister
words of life to a friend.

There are many men whose tongues might govern multitudes if they could govern their tongues.

—George D. Prentice[x]

3 things God hates

There are six things the Lord hates, seven that are detestable to him: haughty eyes, a lying tongue, hands that shed innocent blood, a heart that devises wicked schemes, feet that are quick to rush into evil, a false witness who pours out lies and a man who stirs up dissension among brothers.

Proverbs 6:16-19

Notice that 3 of the 7 things the Lord hates have to do with our mouths.

God says He hates:

A lying tongue. We should ALWAYS speak the truth.

A false witness who pours out lies. God's daughters shouldn't lie about others. We don't want anyone lying about us, right?

A person who sows discord among brothers and sisters. In other words, mind your own business.

Wow! If we know how much the Lord loves us and we know He's given us these warnings for our protection, then we must take heed and ask Him to help us keep our tongue under control. As His girls, our words should be containers of truth and love.

The Lord simply doesn't like gossip. We shouldn't be spreading lies or negative things about others, even if it's true. We always want to help people up, not bring them down.

listen before you gab

Many times, the best preaching and teaching that Christ did was a direct result of listening to someone. People would come to Him with sometimes simple, and other times very difficult, questions. The Holy Spirit would give Jesus the answer every time. James 1:19 tells us to "be quick to listen, slow to speak." A listening heart attracts many friends and will always be rewarded with wisdom from heaven. Here are 4 reasons to have a listening heart.

1. Listening gives you time to fully evaluate a person's situation before you pass on counsel or advice that is premature.

2. Listening tells the person you care. It says that person is important and you are not in a rush to send them away.

3. Listening gives you time to hear from God. The Lord will speak to you clearly when you take unselfish interest in the lives of others.

4. God believes in listening. What do you think He's doing when we pray? He's listening. That's why He gave us 2 ears and 1 mouth: We ought to listen twice as much as we talk.

think pink

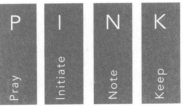

P I N K

Pray | Initiate | Note | Keep

PROVERBS
12 : 15 NLT

Fools think they need no advice,
but the wise listen to others.

Perhaps the most important thing we ever give each other is our attention.... A loving silence often has more power to heal and connect than the most well-intentioned words.

—Rachel Naomi Remen[xi]

3 secrets of a good listener

The Bible says that we are to "be quick to listen, slow to speak" (James 1:19 NIV). Unfortunately, many people are just the opposite and are very quick to speak and extremely slow to listen. When you take the time to listen to somebody, you are showing them that you care and have respect for what they think. It will cement your relationship with that person. What does it take to be a good listener? Here are 3 secrets.

 Look into the eyes of the person you are listening to. This, more than anything, says, "I really do care about what you have to say."

 Think about the point or concern they are sharing. Don't be rehearsing in your mind your answer before you've fully caught all that they are communicating.

 Repeat back a brief synopsis of what they just told you. For example, "Jill, I know you feel sad about not making the team. I believe in you, and if you keep working at it, I think you'll make it next time."

gab with God

Matthew 4:4 NLV says:

But Jesus said, "It is written, 'Man is not to live on bread only. Man is to live by every word that God speaks.'"

God speaks. He gabs, and He created you to gab, too—especially with Him. He knew you before the foundations of the earth. He planned your life in advance.

Ephesians 2:10 AMP says,

For we are God's [own] handiwork (His workmanship), recreated in Christ Jesus, [born anew] that we may do those good works which God predestined (planned beforehand) for us [taking paths which He prepared ahead of time], that we should walk in them [living the good life which He prearranged and made ready for us to live].

God has a specific plan for you. When He speaks to you, take note of it. It may not happen immediately, but when it does, you'll be ready.

If you need direction from God, you can pray this:

Lord, my heart seeks You. I want to do the things that You have already planned for me to do. I'm ready to follow You. I'm waiting to hear Your direction for my life. I want Your best, in Jesus' name.

think pink

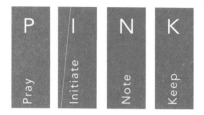

P Pray **I** Initiate **N** Note **K** Keep

Write down the times when you heard God's direction and followed it. What was the outcome? How did you know it was the Lord? It's good to remember the times you heard from God. He is always ready to talk with you.

No heart thrives without much secret converse with God and nothing will make amends for the want of it.

—John Berridge[xii]

listening to God

However, I (Jesus) am telling you nothing but the truth when I say it is profitable (good, expedient, advantageous) for you that I go away. Because if I do not go away, the Comforter (Counselor, Helper, Advocate, Intercessor, Strengthener, Standby) will not come to you [into close fellowship with you]; but if I go away, I will send Him to you [to be in close fellowship with you.]

John 16:7 AMP

Jesus sent the Holy Spirit to fellowship with you. That means he wants to listen to you, answer your questions, give you direction, and help you. But it is tough to receive help from the Lord unless part of your prayer time is spent listening to Him. He wants to tell you specific things about what you are dealing with right now and what is coming in your future. Remember: Anything the Holy Spirit tells you will line up with what the Bible says.

If you want to receive help from the Lord, you can pray this prayer:

Father God, thank You for sending the Holy Spirit to be my counselor and my friend. Help me to make time to listen for Your leading and to follow Your direction, in Jesus' name. Amen.

gab goop

Have you ever made a mess with your gab and had to be forgiven? When your words get you in trouble, God made a way for you to be forgiven and in right standing with Him again.

But if we confess our sins to him, he is faithful and just to forgive us and cleanse us from every wrong.

1 John 1:9 NLT

Everyone makes mistakes and God is so good to have given you a way to receive freedom. This verse was not written to sinners; it was written to Christians. Just because you are saved does not mean you're perfect. God's mercy is here for you right now.

If your gab has made a mess, you can pray this prayer:

Father God, I'm sorry. Forgive me. Thank You for making me clean. Help me to start fresh, in Jesus' name.

think pink

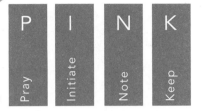

JAMES 4:8 MSG

Say a quiet yes to God and
he'll be there in no time.
Quit dabbling in sin.
Purify your inner life.
Quit playing the field.

Prayer is the great engine to overthrow and rout my spiritual enemies, the great means to procure the graces of which I stand in hourly need.

—John Newton[xiii]

courageous gab

The most courageous thing you can do as you become who you are destined to be is to remain faithful to God. As long as you are okay with God, you are okay with everything else. He is your sounding board. Bounce everything off of Him and get His feedback.

Second Timothy 2:11-13 NKJV says:

> This is a faithful saying: For if we died with Him, we shall also live with Him. If we endure, we shall also reign with Him. If we deny Him, He also will deny us. If we are faithless, He remains faithful; He cannot deny Himself.

People may not always be faithful to you, especially with their words, but God and His Word remain faithful forever.

think pink

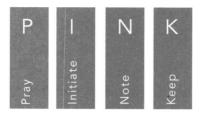

PROVERBS 11 : 30 NLT

The godly are like trees that
bear life-giving fruit, and those
who save lives are wise.

"The very man who has argued you down, will sometimes be found, years later, to have been influenced by what you said."

—C.S. Lewis[xiv]

gab about God

As you grow in your relationship with God, your life will begin to reflect His goodness. Your gab will be filled with thoughts about Him and stories about His faithfulness in your life.

As you gab about God, some people won't want to listen. Some may even try to argue with you. Just remember that you aren't fighting with people; you are fighting the enemy of their souls. (Eph. 6:12.) Pray that God will open doors for you to share His goodness, that He will give you favor in every conversation, and that your friends' spiritual eyes will be opened to the truth.

As you plant word seeds into their lives and pray for them, God will send other believers to water the seeds—and one day you will see the reward of your work when your friends are worshipping God with their lives and words, too.

God bless you and your mouth. I believe with all of my heart that you will use your gab for good!

recommended reading

A Young Woman After God's Own Heart • by Elizabeth George

Girl Talk • by Sheri Rose Shepherd

Girls Of Grace • by Point of Grace

Teenagers Are People Too • by Joyce Meyer

Little Black Books • by Blaine Bartel

For Such a Time as This • by Lisa Ryan

endnotes

i   http://www.quotationspage.com/quote/8544.html

ii   http://www.quotationspage.com/quote/26320.html

iii http://en.thinkexist.com/quotes/frank_outlaw/

iv   http://www.quotationspage.com/quote/27741.html

v   http://www.quotationspage.com/quote/2192.html

vi   *Walking in the Fruit of the Spirit* (Tulsa: Victory Christian Center, 1998).

vii http://www.quotationspage.com/quote/34290.html

viii http://en.thinkexist.com/quotation/wise_men_speak_because_they_have_something_to_say/218003.html

ix   *Single and Loving It* (Tulsa: Harrison House Publishers, 2003) p. 86.

x   http://www.quotationspage.com/quote/9500.html

xi   http://www.wisdomquotes.com/002329.html

xii http://www.cybernation.com/quotationcenter/quoteshow.php?type=author&id=845

xiii http://www.cybernation.com/quotationcenter/quoteshow.php?id=32289

xiv http://en.thinkexist.com/quotes/c.s._lewis/

prayer of salvation

God loves you—no matter who you are, no matter what your past. God loves you so much that He gave His one and only begotten Son for you. The Bible tells us that "...whoever believes in him shall not perish but have eternal life" (John 3:16 NIV). Jesus laid down His life and rose again so that we could spend eternity with Him in heaven and experience His absolute best on earth. If you would like to receive Jesus into your life, say the following prayer out loud and mean it from your heart.

Heavenly Father, I come to You admitting that I am a sinner. Right now, I choose to turn away from sin, and I ask You to cleanse me of all unrighteousness. I believe that Your Son, Jesus, died on the cross to take away my sins. I also believe that He rose again from the dead so that I might be forgiven of my sins and made righteous through faith in Him. I call upon the name of Jesus Christ to be the Savior and Lord of my life. Jesus, I choose to follow You and ask that You fill me with the power of the Holy Spirit. I declare that right now I am a child of God. I am free from sin and full of the righteousness of God. I am saved in Jesus' name. Amen.

If you prayed this prayer to receive Jesus Christ as your Savior for the first time, please contact us on the Web at **www.harrisonhouse.com** to receive a free book.

Or you may write to us at

Harrison House
P.O. Box 35035 • Tulsa, Oklahoma 74153

For more than a quarter of a century, Cathy Bartel has served alongside her husband, Blaine, in what they believe is the hope of the world, the local church. For the better part of two decades, they have served their pastor, Willie George, in building one of America's most respected churches, Church on the Move, in Tulsa, Oklahoma. Most recently, they helped found Oneighty, which has become one of the most emulated youth ministries in the past 10 years, reaching 2,500–3,000 students weekly under their leadership.

While Blaine is known for his communication and leadership skills, Cathy is known for her heart and hospitality. Blaine is quick to recognize her "behind the scenes" gifting to lift and encourage people as one of the great strengths of their ministry together. Her effervescent spirit and contagious smile open the door for her ministry each day, whether she's in the church or at the grocery store.

Cathy is currently helping Blaine raise a new community of believers committed to relevant ministry and evangelism. Northstar Church will open its doors in the growing north Dallas suburb of Frisco, Texas, in the fall of 2006.

Cathy's greatest reward has come in the raising of her 3 boys—Jeremy, 21, Dillon, 19, and Brock, 17. Today, each son is serving Christ with his unique abilities and is deeply involved in Blaine and Cathy's ongoing ministry.

To contact Cathy Bartel please write to:

Cathy Bartel • Serving America's Future
P.O. Box 691923 • Tulsa, Oklahoma 74169
www.blainebartel.com

*Please include your prayer requests
and comments when you write.*

every teen girl's
little pink book

by cathy bartel

daughters are sugar and spice and everything nice...

well, most of the time!

being mommy or daddy's little *princess* can get challenging sometimes. plug into God's Word and discover what it means to be your heavenly Father's daughter and how special you are to your "fam."

stories, humor, scriptures…everything you need to become the lovely and hip *lady* God has destined you to be.

Available at fine bookstores everywhere or at **www.harrisonhouse.com**.

Harrison House
ISBN: 1-57794-792-4

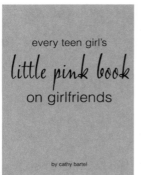

every teen girl's

little pink book

on girlfriends

by cathy bartel

find out how you can be a friend to the end...

girlfriends are great!

- wild and crazy,
- quiet and thoughtful,
- fun and exciting.

you can start being a true "girlfriend" to your gal pals:

learn the ropes

get the inside scoop

navigate clichés

stick together

learn to be real

Available at fine bookstores everywhere or at **www.harrisonhouse.com**.

Harrison House

ISBN: 1-57794-794-0